Whisper of the Anklets
A collection of sixty sonnets

Whisper of the Anklets
A collection of sixty sonnets
Bipin Mohanty

Translated by
Dr. Sonali Sahu

BLACK EAGLE BOOKS
Dublin, USA | Bhubaneswar, India

Black Eagle Books
USA address:
7464 Wisdom Lane
Dublin, OH 43016

India address:
E/312, Trident Galaxy, Kalinga Nagar,
Bhubaneswar-751003, Odisha, India

E-mail: info@blackeaglebooks.org
Website: www.blackeaglebooks.org

First International Edition Published by
Black Eagle Books, 2025

WHISPER OF THE ANKLETS
A collection of sixty sonnets
by Bipin Mohanty
Translated by Dr. Sonali Sahu

Original Copyright © Bipin Mohanty
Translation Copyright © Dr. Sonali Sahu

All rights reserved. No part of this publication may be reproduced, stored in a retrieval system, or transmitted, in any form or by any means, electronic, mechanical, photocopying, recording or otherwise without the prior permission of the publisher.

Cover & Interior Design: Ezy's Publication

ISBN- 978-1-64560-716-8 (Paperback)

Printed in the United States of America

*Dedicated to my dearest Mama,
Mrs. Puspa Mohanty —
the one who may not have given me birth,
but gifted me a new life filled with love, care
and endless affection.*

Translator's Note

Whisper of the Anklets (Paunji Ra Pandulipi) by Bipin Mohanty is not merely a book — it is a lyrical pilgrimage into the soul of rural Odisha. Each of its sixty sonnets resonates with the rhythms of village life: the soft jingle of anklets echoing through narrow earthen lanes, the golden glow of evening lamps lit at the Tulsi shrine, and the ageless serenity of love lived in silence, simplicity, and sacredness.

Composed in the classic Shakespearean sonnet form (4-4-4-2), this collection distills the essence of village emotions — a world where moonlight romances the fields, where glances speak more than words, where rituals cradle relationships, and where even silence carries the weight of longing. These are not merely poems; they are portraits — of a place, a culture, and a heart that beats to the quiet music of belonging.

The sonnets celebrate love in its most unadorned form, the subtle elegance of rural femininity, the spiritual intimacy of shared silences, and the timeless grace woven into everyday moments. At their core lies a deep rootedness — to the soil, to fleeting memories, and to an emotional heritage passed down like heirlooms.

The anklet, in this collection, is not just an ornament; it is a metaphor. It whispers of memory, womanhood, devotion, and legacy — a sound that lingers long after the feet have passed, echoing across generations.

In translating Whisper of the Anklets, my endeavour has been to preserve not only the meaning of each sonnet but the mood — the cadence, the subtle music, the quiet intensity that make Bipin Mohanty's work so richly evocative. This is more than a linguistic bridge; it is an emotional and cultural one.

Whether you come from the heartland of Odisha or are discovering its lyrical traditions for the first time, I hope this collection touches you — allowing you to feel mist-laced mornings, hear voiceless prayers, and walk gently through the tender terrain of these poems.

Whisper of the Anklets is my humble tribute — to poetry, to love, to land, and to the timeless whispers that shape our souls.

Dr. Sonali Sahu
(Translator)

From The Poet's Heart

It gives me immense pleasure to share that my book Paunjira Pandulipi, a collection of sonnets, has been translated into English by Dr. Sonali Sahu under the title 'Whisper of the Anklets'. I am deeply grateful to her for her keen interest and dedication in bringing this work to a wider audience.

I would also like to express my gratitude to Dr. Phani Mohanty, an eminent Indian poet, for his constant guidance and generous support in shaping this work and making this dream a reality.

My heartfelt thanks also go to Mr. Satya Pattnaik, the esteemed publisher of Black Eagle Books, whose humble cooperation and belief in this book made its publication possible. His dedication to literature and his quiet encouragement have been the steady foundation beneath this creative journey.

Bipin Mohanty

CONTENTS

The Filigree of My Love	15
The Love Hour Etched in Time	16
A secret Union With Shadows	17
The Artisan of Konark	18
That Same Anklet, That Same Echo	19
The Lost Anklet	20
Let this Night Never End	21
The Regret of The Anklet	22
The Grief of a Youthful Night	23
That is My Last Love	24
A Teasing Breeze of Chaitra Spring	25
A Selfie With a Kiss	26
The Moon of Your Village	27
Fainting Melody	28
The Vanished Anklet	29
Let Our Love Be Alive	30
Where Has It Gone	31
Beloved and The Anklet	32
Woman and The Fire	33
Two Birds of Love	34
Will Attain Nirvana Smilingly	35
Wanderer of The Evening	36
Lyrics of Tears	37
False Promise	38
Wine-filled Clay Pot	39
Dwell in Me, and I In You	40
Light of Hope	41
Forbidden Rendezvous	42
The Temple Tower of Our Village	43
The Serene Cold of My Village	44
If Only You Had Come	45

Anklet From Cuttack	46
Love You Deeply	47
The Sacred Script of Love	48
The Defeat of Life	49
What Poem Is It ?	50
Same Footsteps, Same Melody	51
Her Jingling Anklets	52
Letter of Fallen Leaves	53
Poetic Beauty	54
Who Is There That Has'nt Been Burned !	55
Darling	56
Dream House	57
Desired Union	58
The Clay Pot Melts into Earth	59
Love is Bought and Sold Here	60
The Martyr is Returning	61
Ah! Once a Poet Lived	62
An Anklet's Tale	63
Give Me Back	64
Confession	65
Who is That Compassionate Poet ?	66
A Test of Tears	67
The First Melody of a New Bride's Anklet	68
The First Sin	69
A Bit of a Time Remains	70
That Day, Those Anklets	71
Anklet Vs Ghungroo	72
The Drizzle From Your Village	73
Sleep Has Fled My Village	74

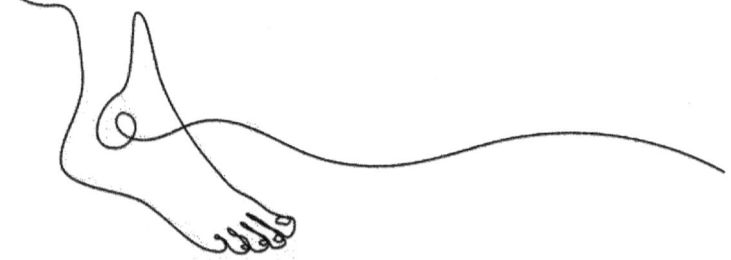

The Filigree of My Love

From Chandni Chowk I brought an anklet bright,
It chimed with grace upon your tender feet.
Through Cuttack's lanes I roamed by day and night,
Your smile once made my aching soul complete.

Two anklets hum the dreams I dared to own,
They breathe in silence, never fading far.
Is it the moon, or anklet's secret tone,
Or both your feet that shame like starlight scar?

They tiptoe through the dark with silver sound,
The song is heard by Jhuma Didi too.
The village gossips, envy burns around,
They shame your feet for what they never knew.

In Cuttack's maze, where lanes and markets gleam,
Even lost anklets echo love's old dream.

The Love Hour Etched In Time

Who walks with feet that hush my breath,
A silver anklet sings of love and death.
In silent nights, her gestures flame my chest,
Urvashi descends — my soil, her sacred nest.

I'm a lost lover who shivers at her chime.
A shadow of fear haunts my soul each time.
Nights slipped away with her anklet in my head.
I found the tavern — and never returned, I said.

My evenings fade in wine and her anklet's gleam,
In silence, her chime halts my life's bright dream.
I burn like a lamp in a juggler's lost game,
Each night I die — each dawn, life calls my name.

I plead today — I'm the merchant of her anklet's sound,
In this silent world, your voice poisons all around.

A Secret Uninon With Shadows

I have a pact with the darkness, O darling, come near,
Turn away the light waiting quietly at the door, dear.
Let your Krishna-black tresses shed the jasmine tight,
Let your silk saree slip, like a whisper in the night.

Cast off the jewel of shame, let modesty fall,
Hold me close in the silence of your arms' call.
Don't save this night for dreams alone to keep,
Swear me seven lives—but no more lies beneath.

Wrap your bare body gently into mine,
I'll kiss your soul in darkness, line by line.
Don't sit and weep in the corner of light's home,
In this sacred shrine of life, love is a tender wrong.

Let a single night quench the thirst of countless lives,
On a new map of earth, we'll script where history thrives.

The Artisan of Konark

Offer your brimming cup to my lips, my darling,
Let this mad tavern taste the wine of loving.
Let the night fulfill its silent, burning desire,
This beauty has made pride's plea expire.

Let echoes rest within these glassy walls,
Let shadows drift as silent slumber falls.
Let love arise in mahuli's sweet haze,
While Chandrabhaga glows in silk-lit rays.

Let your Krishna-dark hair fall loose by the wall,
Let madhumalti's fragrance drift through all.
Let morning stars fade, let birdsong disappear,
And let our shadows dance on Konark's carved frontier.

Let a stranger's touch awaken my sleeping eyes,
So I may break your embrace and see the first sunrise.

That Same Anklet, That Same Echo

The anklet on your feet sings the very same tune,
For which this mad lover loses her way too soon.
One night, I tore through the darkness so deep,
Guided by your voice, to the place where you sleep.

That night was a canvas, a melody, a hall of hues,
You came, heavy-footed, with a brimming glass
My eyes caught your anklet — my drink slipped away,
And with its jingling rhythm, I drifted in a drunken sway.

There's no wine in the drink, my sweet,
Your bare feet pulled me into heat.
Come close and let the night begin,
I'll loose your anklet, dim the flame within.

I can't tell the drink from the drunk I become,
Your blushing lips, to mine, I softly welcome.

The Lost Anklet

Ah, let your anklet be lost once more on your left side,
At dusk, you'd sit by the river, lips folded in a silent tide.
Alone, yet with you, I'd join the hush you wore,
Together we'd search for what the silence had in store.

That excuse of a search—how deeply we'd disappear,
Soaked in night's hush, with no shade of fear.
For love is no sin, not in the dark nor light,
Your open eyes chasing that anklet in fading sight.

You'd loosen your tight blouse, shyly meeting my gaze,
Calling me "naughty," asking I help in tender ways.
If only I had, perhaps the anklet wouldn't vanish again,
And your leaving wouldn't echo in every refrain.

Life is made to lose, to find, then lose once more—
So come, let's misplace that anklet like before.

Let This Night Never End

After dusk, my footsteps find your door once more,
Like a wanderer lost, yet to your home I'm sure.
Each evening I sip from the earthen cup you keep,
A nectar not of wine, but memories rich and deep.

From crowds I slip, for just two sips I crave,
And speak my heart, no longer shy or brave.
On the unsteady path of night, I fall, I sway,
Yet who is mine or not, the colors blur away.

My soul sings in a void dressed in desire's hue,
Bathed in kisses once tasted, tender and true.
The feast of your touch, the warmth of your grace,
A goblet of love, not wine, held in your embrace.

If such is the thrill in the taste of your flame,
Then pour me love's cup—let this dry life be tamed.

The Regret Of The Anklet

This tired night lies scattered in love's embrace,
Jasmine falls, perfuming the silent space.
Your loosened hair floats like clouds in flight,
After love's war, silence owns the night.

A broken anklet rests, far from its pair,
The right foot trembles, touched by whispered air.
How do you bear my sorrow, soft and still—
While I dissolve in love's relentless will?

Leaning close, the left foot dares to speak:
"You were too wild in love's shadowed peak."
The night retreats from anklet's bold reply,
Its chime now breaks the hush we held so high.

Bound in both feet, dark dreams took their flight—
Yet fate denied our arms this silent night.

The Grief of a Youthful Night

By evening's touch, my body burns with a fire untamed,
I slip away unseen, my anguish never named.
My feet move ahead, yet shadows drag me behind,
Till I reach the chamber where her hands offer wine.

Two drops touch my lips — a royal trance begins,
My mouth speaks of kingdoms, of pleasures and sins.
She loosens her anklet, binds ghungroos tight with pride,
And the night shimmers, awakened by her stride.

In mujra's dance, my madness gently fades,
I know how to lose myself while mind still stays.
With the wine and the one who pours it, I never fight,
I sip melody to melody deep into the night.

The dancer's feet never tire — her rhythm is my cure,
For this wild youth, dear sir, my habits I endure.

This Is My Last Love

I will not beg for sleep from shattered dreams,
Nor crave Chandrabhaga's moonlit beams.
Not for your heart, nor lips that hide the sky—
No longer will I question how or why.

I'll seek you in the night's enchanted grace,
In silent corners love forgot to trace.
Where shadows hum and honeyed secrets lie,
Beneath your walls, where sweeter echoes sigh.

I won't trade you for incense in the air,
Or barter you for time that we could share.
No fading hope shall steal you once again,
No trance shall blur the truth or birth my pain.

Forgive this heart, so lost and yet so true—
For all of time, my last love is you.

A Teasing Breeze Of Chaitra Spring

You are the living whisper of my verdant dream,
The enchanting melody of my shadowed stream.
You are the silent tale in my breathless nights,
The stolen glance in spring's soft bites.

You are the naughty Fagun night that flirts with flowers,
The unknown love of a girl in flickering towers.
You are the pride of the Yamuna's youthful tide,
The tremble of my heart where kadamb trees hide.

You are the longing of mad spring in sorrow's sway,
The regret of a dusk where joy fades away.
You are the bashful blush of my star-kissed skies,
The garden of care where my silence lies.

O beloved, let me adorn your hair with vermilion red—
This love-crazed soul has little time ahead.

A Selfie with a Kiss

I sent the moon to rest upon your sill,
To speak our hearts when all the world is still.
It placed a kiss with care upon your hand,
And said, "He sends his heart—please understand."

But yours I won't let sail through moonlit skies,
It plays too wild, with mischief in its eyes.
The kiss I sent last time was led astray,
A thousand lips had snatched it on the way.

What came returned was faint, too torn to keep—
I drank it down with tears I couldn't weep.
This time your kiss will come to me direct,
Folded in trust no thief would dare suspect.

And don't forget—a selfie with that bliss,
Your smile that breaks my chest—I won't miss.

The Moon of Your Village

The honeybee from your village showed me sweet,
It led me through where madhu malti meet.
The breeze from there stole off with all my mind,
In parijat of love, my soul did unwind.

Each time your village blooms at dusk's soft hue,
I whisper out your name—the sky hears too.
The kohl that lines your gaze was born from grace,
When night lifts there, my moon begins its chase.

At dusk, the moon returns through smoky haze,
My village sinks in love's unspoken phase.
Your sari slips while you fix strands of hair,
And back you come with silence, soft and bare.

One day, the line between our homes will stray—
And you'll light Tulsi's lamp at end of day.

Fainting Melody

I brought fine anklets from old Cuttack's lane,
My soulmate's sister watched, with curiosity plain,
To gift my playful love, my heart's delight.
Then snatched them quick, her eyes aglow with light.

She slipped them on and asked, "Do these look fair?"
Upon her feet, so pale and soft and bare.
I froze—a truth hung heavy in the air—
She charmed me more than I would ever dare.

Those bells like whispers rang on marble cold,
Her glance held dreams too tender to be told,
As filigree in silent stone would gleam.
More haunting than a sculptor's broken dream.

Yet I, a lover, could not ask them back—
Her eyes held stars my soul would always lack.

The Vanished Anklet

Thy anklet lost again? A strange refrain,
Not once, but seven times it's gone astray.
A game, perchance, that dances in thy brain—
To hide it so, and steal my peace away.

For in thy anklet lives my heart's own thread,
Each chime recalls the beat I feel for thee.
Yet every time it slips, I'm filled with dread,
As if our tale drifts off too easily.

Thou speak'st to me in shadows of the night,
Confessions whispered soft in twilight's veil.
But jest though make of love and lost delight,
And call this night to drink from passion's grail.

Thy feet I watch, to read what's left unsaid—
To find the anklet... and be near thee led.

Let Our Love Be Alive

I adore the silent sound your anklet sings at night,
When darkness trembles as it trips with anklet's flight.
Leaning on my chest, you ask me of the moon's abode,
Where stars and moon in bridal bonds together glowed.

Your anklet hides when you see me — perhaps not by chance,
You lose it knowingly, within your teasing glance.
Our tale of love is whispered through the village air,
How many noons you've played this game with secret care.

You lose your anklet just to softly speak with me,
In its search, your heart reveals what others can't see.
I know you're seeking me when it goes astray —
They call me "lover of anklet's lost ballet."

Let this anklet be lost, once more or two —
But let our love remain alive and true.

Where Has It Gone?

Where has it gone — the pondside bath in algae's green?
Where is that girl on stones by rivers seen?
Where has it gone — dusk's beauty in her pleated dress?
Where is her foot on stone, scrubbing with tenderness?

Where is the anklet's chime, the bridal grace once near?
Where is that waist, the pot she held so dear?
Where is the garland — jasmine, champa in her hair?
Where is that girl who left the world without a care?

Where is the sari on her rain-soaked frame so shy?
Where are the eyes that read my heart, then passed by?
Where is that first love, that heartbeat's secret song?
Where are her feet with alta, soft and strong?

Where is the love beneath her bashful veil once lit?
Where is that kiss — that new bride's memory, bit by

Beloved and the Anklet

Beloved and her anklet — why return this way?
When once my youth in her deep love would play.
She's no more that lover, nor her anklet's beat,
Yet shame still walks with me through every street.

If love was wrong — that wrong I chose to bear,
If sin it was, why must I still despair?
Let such a love live on through flame and age,
Let slander come — I hold no shame nor rage.

She stained my name, yet made me whole again,
I rose, a victor, through love's fiercest pain.
From Kashmir down to Kanyakumari flows
My tale of love — where every witness knows:

To live unloved is fire, not sweet desire—
But lovers win through sacred, burning fire.

Woman and the Fire

I am a great yogi, lost in words of sacred art,
In me, O love, you stirred a vowless, celibate heart.
I knew not then that woman and fire burn the same,
Touching flame or you — my faith stood firm, my claim.

Mohini! You broke my trance, bound me in your snare,
Like Rishyashringa's child chasing the goat with care.
No peaks rise higher than your lifted breast's delight,
This love, this wild surge, rose at that very sight.

In your cheek's dimple sleeps the ocean's grace,
This sinner finds his dwelling in that very place.
She holds my heart in her palm, and softly speaks—
For her, to play with fire is no mighty feat.

Love is never desire, nor pleasure of the mind—
But faith drowned in fire, and detachment left behind.

Two Birds of Love

My eyes burn blue — come, beloved, be mine.
Your tongue drips full — I'll drink it dry,
No weight like yours, no lover like I.

I sipped your poison, turned divine —
Now Neelkanth, with your soul in mine.
You wrapped yourself into my skin,
Your serpent self begins to spin.

Your sari slips, your mark revealed,
In shadowed dark, what fate's unsealed?
I kiss your feet, your sacred sign,
I'm caught where waist and wonder twine.

Sin and virtue — two wings of flame,
You hold the pure, I hold the blame.

Will Attain Nirvana Smilingly

I'm no mere monk in robes — I'm love's great sage.
They mock me still, a fake — but love writes my page.
Where flesh begins to speak, I turn away,
Is love not more than flesh, than lust's decay?

The forest must be set in blazing fire,
This body too must feel that deep desire.
One who walks through flame in flesh and breath—
Only he has known love's sacred death.

From union, parting — one fire will arise,
Cowards fear its blaze and mask their cries.
Only the burned can speak of pain so true,
Without deep sadhana, who ever knew?

Come, let us burn — and smiling, touch Nirvana.
For love's one spark, we'll give our life's pramana.

Wanderer Of The Evening

The bee from your village showed me where to sweet,
Through woods where madhu malti and fragrance meet.
The breeze from there slipped softly through my mind,
Among your parijat, my soul stayed behind.

When blooms arise with dusk in quiet light,
I call your name into the falling night.
The kohl that lines your eyes outshines the rest,
When darkness lifts, my moon begins its jest.

As twilight folds the day, the pale moon glows,
My village soaks in love the silence knows.
Your sari slips while you fix windswept hair,
You walk back slow — regret upon the stair.

One day, the lines between our homes will part—
You'll light Tulsi's lamp deep in my heart.

Lyrics of Tears

Why does the past return so deep today?
The distant road now seems to come my way.
What I had to say—I left unsaid,
What I had to do remains half-dead.

I came with nothing, and with none shall go,
But sindoor and your alta—let them show.
Till I burn, these two bangles will remain,
Let the mridang beat through smoke and pain.

If your anklets sound not that mournful night,
Place them on my feet for the final rite.
When flames consume me, bring them back once more—
They're love's last relic, what my soul still wore.

That anklet knows my tears and bleeding truth,
Weep in its glow, and recall love's lost youth.

False Promise

Wait, don't go—the dream isn't over yet,
The night still lingers, let your image stay and set.
Let me spend this dark with the sight of your frame,
Wear those anklets, tie your hair—ignite the flame.

Lift the slipped saree, cover your form once more,
Step into my room like you've done before.
Softly place your feet on the floor so still,
Let me see your face, beyond eyelids' will.

Through your deep sleep I feel your presence near,
Like a shy deer's touch that draws me clear.
If I opened my eyes, I'd hold you tight,
A tiger asleep won't miss its prey at night.

Your playful slip away, your naughty retreat—
A sacred sin played out so sweet.
My love in dreams, soaked in silent delight,
A false promise echoes in this shadowed night.

Wine-filled Clay Pot

Place the clay pot filled with wine inside the tavern,
Come quickly—don't be late like every time again.
Bring just a bouquet of paper flowers for me,
But this time, don't bring the sweet pain of a rose.

On that night of darkness, light shall dwell,
The deep night will be swallowed by deeper hell.
I'll call the moon, summon the stars to stay,
Steal sky's blue and your love that day,

With every sip, the night will slowly end,
Drunk in love, I'll cherish your chest, my friend.
My feet may wander here and there in desire,
But love for you will never tire.

Before you leave, read my heart and give a kiss—
That kiss will be my last… that night, my final bliss.

Dwell in Me, and I in You

Come, my beloved—let this night soak in your love,
Fill the cup with wine, let us drink till the stars above.
Unbutton your blouse, let down that bluish braid,
Enclose me within you, for this night, let fears fade.

Where darkness meets more darkness, love still yearns,
True love glows, unafraid of what the world discerns.
Let not even the stars cast their gaze so wide—
Someone may be listening, standing on the other side.

Silent and senseless, our union blooms tonight,
What lover could watch and not burst with fright?
Only an artist, in dreams, could craft such a key—
But without sensing pulse, he knows not intimacy.

Let our love live quietly, hidden deep inside,
Lest some sculptor carves us in stone with pride.

Light of Hope

The jingle of your anklet hums like song,
Its sound alone can shatter me all wrong.
One anklet near—my soul feels not its own,
Yet love's two syllables die overthrown.

It's not just metal—but sorrow dressed in grace,
What's left of life now clings in breathless place.
A day without its chime—my heart turns weak,
That anklet wounds far more than words you speak.

It sings my song, its tune my silent cry,
Without its echo, bonds feel hard to tie.
From anklet to sleep, to dreams, to sacred vow,
Each night it leaves the dark with echoes now.

In this empty life, I chase its shining trace—
Its sound alone lends my soul lasting grace.

Forbidden Rendezvous

Don't drive me mad this aging afternoon,
Drunk for days beneath a reeling moon.
Sip by sip, I've drowned in wine so deep,
Yet one more cup brings neither peace nor sleep.

This night, that night—what's left to compare?
I drank back then, I drink now—same despair.
Your love's the sky—too vast for me to hold,
Yet what I saw today turned brave to cold.

My eyes now stray, my feet can barely stand,
Hold me close—this night slips from my hand.
Bind me in your arms till the haze is through,
Then I'll return—soft, silent, back to you.

Just guide me home, no matter how I seem—
Not as your lover, but a drunk lost in a dream.

The Temple Tower of Our Village

Your village riverbank, mustard fields aglow,
My village's bees pour love in golden flow.
A girl from yours sways with a pot in grace,
While my butterflies slip through hands in chase.

At dusk, your lily gazes at our moon,
Who blooms in your sky, forgetting omen too soon.
Your proud peahen twirls before our cloud's eye,
And our cloud rains on your fields, drifting by.

As Tulsi lamps glow in our evening air,
A flower falls from your Tarini's hair.
Our bride walks wearing anklets from your place,
While your red bindi hides in our vermilion's grace.

Spring comes in secret where our paths align—
Your joy, my shrine—two hearts in one design.

The Serene Cold of My Village

The cold is mustard fields by our river's bend,
The anklet's song on feet that never end.
It's women gathered where the riverside flows,
And elders' lips where December quietly shows.

The cold is the smile of fields in golden bloom,
The dawn-lit hearth that crackles through the gloom.
It's rangoli my mother draws with loving grace,
And temple bells that echo into twilight's space.

The cold is a moonlit night wrapped in dark,
The mango tree shedding blossoms soft and stark.
It's harvested grain in silence stacked with pride,
And mother's blue sari swaying outside.

As sun breaks through, her rangoli shines bright—
And the waist-wrap stirs in winter's morning light.

If Only You Had Come

If only you had come, and brought back youth's flame,
We'd sit beneath the moon, freed from all shame.
Light here, shadow there, and doubt between—
Shall I be saint or lover—pure or obscene?

If only you gave the moon its glow once more,
And silvered night returned to sky and shore.
Had you returned my youth, slowed age's race,
Who finds truth now—Baula or tiger's face?

Who gives up silence with the dark so deep?
A coward or a lover strays like sheep.
Your black hair floats like cloud in sky's wide grace,
But without rain, even clouds lose their place.

The night of youth fades fast, beloved—see,
Let madness play, and set this moment free.

Anklet from Cuttack

No one should love like this—such is my fate,
She pouts in silence for anklets, small and great.
She sent a photo—asked how it should be,
Our names engraved in love, between anklets three.

I roamed through Cuttack—each lane, each bend,
From Baniapati to Bakshi, without end.
But the filigree charm I knew was gone,
Just names remain, in shows that drag on.

A toe ring I brought, not the anklet she asked,
"Let your foot wear this," I said, gently masked.
But she stomped in rage, face flushed with pride,
"No anklet? Then goodbye!"—and walked aside.

At last, from Khimji I got the perfect pair—
She laughed, "Next time, bring Cuttack's flair."

Love you Deeply

I love you deeply—yet words can't convey,
For fear the world may steal our light someday.
What if their gaze casts shadows on our flame?
How long can love survive beneath such blame?

There's none like you—so radiant, so rare,
Even the moon is flawed—it wouldn't dare .
You're heaven-sent, divinely bright and true,
No beauty in this world compares to you.

How many nights must dreams hold you near?
In silence, I close my eyes—both peace and fear.
Let this one life stay sacred, still, and pure,
For even seven births may not ensure.

If you ever stand where my silence sleeps,
Whisper—our love, beyond this world, still keeps.

The Sacred Script Of Love

You sleep now in death's soft bed,
I long for a glance unsaid.
Krushnachuda burns in flame,
Even summer speaks your name.

These eyes missed your lovely face,
So close—yet time gave no grace.
When did you walk in so still?
Were those the feet I'd thrill?

Anklets, bangles, sindoor bright,
Now fade in funeral light.
O kin, I beg—don't let them burn,
Let those anklets please return.

We vowed for seven lives to stay,
But death has turned love away.

The Defeat of Life

Regret of hope now fills my plea,
A half-lived dream, half memory.
I asked the moon for gentle light,
The earth for clay—both lost from sight.

In wholeness, emptiness took hold,
The one I loved turned distant, cold.
Some gave me pain, some silent cries,
No questions asked, no need for whys.

Through thorns and fire, I walked alone,
Wore cursed tears like a crown of stone.
I've lived through storms, through every strain—
But death's escape is not my lane.

I fear no end, nor bend to strife,
A warrior stands till last of life.

What Poem Is It ?

What poem is it, if it speaks not of the soul of the soil?
What verse omits Kalinga's courage, born of toil?
What poem forgets a craftsman's sacred skill and grace?
What poem ignores the stone's own tale etched on its face?

What poem is it that has never sung of spring's delight?
What verse lacks love and passion burning bright?
What kind of poem leaves out the stars' radiant gleam?
And where's the poetry if a butterfly's love isn't dreamed?

What poem is it that speaks not of revolution's flame?
Where the foe stood tall, and never bowed in shame?
What verse forgets to speak of peace?
Can untouched war make poems cease?

If I don't write such verses, then I am no poet at all,
A poet is a creator, a seer, who feels every rise and fall.

Same Footsteps, Same Melody

Whose anklet echoes like it's part of me,
It dances near, then hides where none can see.
It hums in dreams, then quietly disappears,
Now laughs with joy, now melts into soft tears.

I've felt it—her anklet dancing in my yard,
In winter, spring, and rains, it strikes me hard.
Its rhythmic song drives all my senses wild,
Who is this beauty who loves me like a child?

The same anklet, the same tune—my life has passed ,
In her soap-scented sari, she feels like spring in full display.
She colors my dreams, fills my eyes with restful night,
Whose anklet is this, whose melody the stars try to imitate

Two anklets on your feet are love's rare stone,
I live this life, knowing well—you're not my own.

Her Jingling Anklets

Who is this girl whose anklet sings?
Whose feet hold such divine-like wings?
She's stolen sleep from these tired eyes,
And left me lost beneath the skies.

Whose feet now wear such gentle grace?
Who left me by the stream—no trace.
A piece of moon fell by the stream,
Not anklet—but her laugh in gleam.

Who carved such velvet gold so bright?
From Rambha's line, or Menaka's light?
I found her anklet—won't give it away,
It haunts my thoughts by night and day.

I tied it on Radha's feet, so fair—
Such grace as hers is rare, so rare.

Letter of Fallen Leaves

On fallen leaves, I wrote a note to Spring,
A final plea—come soon, let swiftness bring.
This form is dimmed—just brush me as you pass,
Once, your touch set fire beneath my glass.

In new form, I shall bloom and rise again,
We'll call the winds, invite the storm and rain.
The world shall watch us etch a burning name,
Where youth still hides beneath the autumn flame.

Let time turn back—we'll dare to love once more,
Though judged as wrong, we'll open love's old door.
The heart may tire, but love won't fade or die—
It only climbs with age, toward the sky.

I scattered stars, believing you would stay,
Now wrapped in dark, I wait night and day.

Poetic Beauty

How much pain must one bear to give a poem birth?
A poet chases words from dusk to dawn on earth.
He steals starlight, moon-glow, colors from the sky,
Wraps them in love and lets them softly sigh.

At times, a poem mourns a maiden's silent eyes,
Or fills a tavern's cup with echoed cries.
It borrows half a song from someone's dream,
Or lights a bride's first night with hope's warm gleam.

The universe's key blooms in the poet's gaze,
Sometimes in tears, or hunger's aching blaze.
He doesn't just write—he lives what words conceal,
Where thought and fire and silence gently kneel.

He builds an empire of love, vast and true,
Where beauty dances in ruin's glowing hue.

Who is there that hasn't been Burned!

A year has passed since your quiet goodbye,
Yet you feign no change beneath open sky.
"Love needs no tongue," the poet once had sighed,
To the poet's quill, my soul still replied.

Your silence lingers, cold as passing air,
The shift in time you still refuse to bear.
A flame once sparked, still flickers in the night,
While you walk on, untouched by its dim light.

Love is a dance of dark and blazing light,
The lamp's a mask that hides consuming might.
The moth dives in, deceived by fire's face,
And burns with grace — not shame, nor a disgrace.

This forest learns through fire's cruel desire,
For love is pain that sets the soul on fire.

Darling

To love, I bow from far — my land now calls to me,
The foes have gathered close, beyond the border's sea.
Place tilak on my head, then smile and bid goodbye,
Let me take your last kiss, for my nation, I'll die.

Let foes now face the fire that our love can hold,
More fierce than atom's wrath, more fearless and bold.
Let bullets kiss my chest and bloom a rose,
Where your name was, now my nation glows.

If I fall at the front, don't cry behind the veil,
Just wipe your crimson love, and smile beyond the pale.
No tears shall wet the flag that wraps me when I rest,
For that's my mother's veil, now lying on my chest.

No pact with cowardice, no peace with trembling breath,
Sing brave the song of love that dares to dance with death.

Dream House

Your silent lips stir storms in my chest,
I built no home—never thought it best.
This is how I live, and how I'll stay,
Even birds find leaves to nest and pray.

Still, no one stops the dreamer's flight,
But without you, dreams lose their light.
A stolen moon slips into my room,
While anklets echo in soft perfume.

I dreamed a home on a branch so bare,
Wrapped in silence left by stormy air.
How can I break what once was mine?
Like dusk's lost bird, I call you divine.

The crowd grows loud, but I miss you still,
Guarding memories no night can kill.

Desired Union

Upon the bed, the garlands fall—
Champa, jasmine, one and all.
Night jasmine sighs, "My fate is brief,"
While jasmine asks, "Who grants relief?"

The gardener plucks with tender grace,
But who recalls the neck or face?
The path is red with blood and name,
Yet wedding nights still smell the same.

As flowers bloom, the wings take flight—
Men break their vows, then vanish from sight.
This forest holds unspoken cries,
No one asks where sorrow lies.

O gardener, vow and scatter me
Where brave hearts walk in victory.

The Clay Pot Melts into Earth

One day the clay will fade to dust,
All wealth and pride betray your trust.
This "mine, mine" cry is hollow sound,
Even your pyre won't stay around.

In glittered eyes, I drank love's wine,
Believed in death, if love was mine.
That death, so rare, I've long endured—
A puppet, lost, love's pain ensured.

In night's soft lap, I touched your skin,
Yet her shadow still dwells within.
Who knows what jasmine dares confess?
Even Nandan bows to such finesse.

Your lips meet mine—yet in this flame,
My anklet weeps, still calling your name.

Love Is Bought And Sold Here

On my wedding night, I lit no sacred lamp's glow,
Nor questioned past love's sins I used to know.
I've lived this life a stranger to love's true call,
And built my home by passion's guarded river wall.

Here night falls, and bright feasts of desire arise,
The courtesan's anklets make even the night dance in disguise.
Flowers fall from her hair, her dress slips to the floor—
Love is mocked and sold, behind a price-tagged door.

The heart never knows when its love departs,
Why expose a true love and tear it apart?
Let this city of hate rise, yet sweetness stay,
How long is the road I walk in dismay?

Where's the give and take of a love not found here?
In this world of sale and trade, even love couldn't steer clear.

The Martyr Is Returning

I promised you, Mother, I'd return one day,
Now see—my coffin comes from war's harsh fray.
A martyr I am, in pride I now reside,
This land salutes your motherhood worldwide.

I sleep now wrapped in the Tricolor's fold,
A shower of petals as farewells unfold.
With cannon salutes, my journey finds rest,
The flag bows low—your son gave his best.

Let no tears fall from your sacred eyes,
You raised a son whom the nation glorifies.
Have you seen a death more grand, more bright?
Your sacrifice now burns a guiding light.

May this land bear sons both brave and true,
And mothers strong—just like you.

Ah ! Once a poet lived

After I die, they'll say, "A poet once lived here,"
Who conquered foes and hearts with verses clear.
But none will speak of how he truly bled,
To them, his life was joy, not tears he shed.

He lived ignoring the world's cruel disguise,
Promising to write what still in silence lies.
If granted just a few more borrowed days,
He'd make love beneath her blue hair's gaze.

He never feared death, nor bowed his face—
In poems, he lived, and died with grace.
For him, death's fear was not to chase—
A poet dies, but not with ease or trace.

The poet's soul, immortal in each breath,
So why should one cry at his quiet death?

An Anklet's Tale

My anklet rings soft 'rum-jhum' upon the feet,
In village yards, my dreams are lost every day.
Once I would dance, lost in festive delight,
Even farmers would hum within their fields.

A goldsmith shaped me with utmost care,
Carved and etched, molded with loving hands.
Through flame and fire I was tempered well,
Forgetting all pain, I embraced a happy life.

On a dancer's feet I chime across the floor,
On a lover's feet I whisper songs of love.
With a new bride I walk shyly, step by step,
Through midnight darkness, I make the room glow.

My fate is tied to Madhvi's sacred tavern,
My feet bear both virtue and sin as offerings.

Give Me Back

Give me my childhood, those golden days,
That restless heart, those playful ways.
Give back her lap, the half-moon's shine,
The saree's edge where tears met mine.

Give me my hut, the old home's grace,
The Tulsi bell, that sacred place.
Bring back the love I left behind,
The village gate to heaven aligned.

Return the gourds and siuli bloom,
The anklet's song in evening gloom.
Bring back the chants, the holy crowd,
The Gita's light, Bhanja's voice proud.

Let me hear once more that sacred song,
And winter mist where fields belong.

Confession

Your serene face shines like a sacred shrine,
With sandalwood's faint breath your being swells,
A lamp that burns to give its light is thine,
Though 'neath its glow the shadow darkly dwells.

Through worlds of hunger, grief, and want you stepped,
Through bonds of need you wove a magic tie,
In orphaned arms my pride and will you kept,
With loving balm you stilled the wounded cry.

Through threads of sweat and tears you made your way,
Through tattered cloth and meals you could not claim,
With steadfast heart you bore the weight each day,
A beacon 'mid the mist of doubt and shame.

Through stubborn strife the bitter past must fall,
Your light shines forth to guide and warm us all.

Who is that compassionate poet ?

I run after words every morning with a hopeful heart,
I float upon the ocean of feelings, making my start.
Though I try to teach this proud poem, it slips away,
What song can I write that the world will call mine one day?

I beg the flower, "Color my heart with love and glee."
It snaps, "Don't touch—you're just a lewd butterfly to me!"
The honeybee drank its fill and forgot its own way,
How many came and left as lovebirds flew away?

From Sasmita to Rita, from Mita, Sita, and Gita too,
Through this word called 'love', I found moments so few.
What can I write of this pride I carry within?
The dream to be a poet may never truly begin.

And who will sigh and say with a heart deeply swayed,
"Ah! He too was a poet, in times long decayed"?

A Test of Tears

My darling, veil not this midnight hour,
Slip the anklets from your feet, let silence reign;
Let wine abide, its warmth to overpower,
Before this final night of youth must wane.

Through dance, your footsteps spoke to claim my heart,
Through mist I sought life 'neath your fragrant braid;
Let flame consume the lamp, its sacred part,
While faintly shines a teardrop, half–conveyed.

A pearl of grief rests shy within your eye,
A lover knows to veil such bitter gleam;
Though you call me drunkard, I can't belie,
For love can trace sweat and tear in its dream.

Give me your honeyed kiss in place of pain,
And hide me 'gainst your breast this night, again.

The First Melody of a New Bride's Anklet

The bride's first anklet rings soft and clear,
She scrubs her feet by the pond, friends near.
Laughter glows on lips the tides envy,
Her beauty outshines every deity.

Whose crescent rests by the river at night,
With jasmine hair and skin like misty light?
How long can this stone bear her silent grace,
As youth's weight deepens on its aching face?

Longing's gold gnaws quietly at the core,
Her foot slips where moss lines the shore.
She dives through mist, soaked and divine,
A sculptor waits, still reading the sign.

Love's mark is not for fleeting desire—
But a lifetime's chain, forged in fire.

The First Sin

Someone stole an anklet from Patia Chowk one night,
More than an ornament, it was the ledger of a first sin.
The whole village whispers you're somehow different,
Whose lustful gaze claimed that anklet within?

How could such a heavy anklet suddenly break?
Whose hands would use it, and for what sake?
Lost in a midnight feast, a drunken mist,
You swayed like Madhubala, too dazed to resist.

They found it later in Manua's hands, they say,
Its soft jhum-jhum wakes the village each day.
My heart swears it was he who claimed that prize,
With a blackened face, he still remembers the night's cries.

If you must take the other anklet too, then go,
But grant me a faint memory before the crimson flow.

A Bit of a Time Remains

Come, let us start our love anew,
A chance meeting in some unknown town.
In your silvery beauty, my gaze will rest,
A fresh line of poetry rising in my chest.

My hungry eyes will return to you again and again,
While you, shyly, draw lines with your toes, head bowed.
A fragrant spring will rise from deep within you,
Whispering, "This is the sign of first love."

That day, we'll wander the whole city,
Searching for lost memories, for feelings long buried.
You've placed no sindoor for anyone, nor have I wed,
What a dry, lonely love for which life is bet?

Love is a friend worth countless lifetimes,
Come, let us burn in its flame of union tonight

That Day, Those Anklets

Beside the green and whispering river's side,
A lone green angel cleansed her anklet bright;
One gone, she sighed as dusk began to glide,
And misty moons emerged to claim the night.

We met upon the path, your pouted face,
A springtime flame that blushed the midnight air;
"My anklet lost," you sighed with shy disgrace,
"They'll shame me soon, those elders in their care."

"Then wait," I spoke, "by this deserted shore,
Through mist and dusk I'll seek what fate has spun."
I searched until the silver bell I bore,
And placed it back, as moons and stars were one.

Though bare one foot, no path felt torn apart,
For fate had bound an anklet to my heart.

Anklet Vs Ghungroo

In crowded halls, wine and the server play,
Feet stumble—Madhubala sleeps midway.
The tavern glows, the drink commands its hold,
A clay jug falls, the cupbearer lies cold.

The dancer's ghungroo snaps, scattered on ground,
The anklet says, "Rise up—let dance resound!"
The Nawab's drunk, fed, sprawled on velvet spread,
The ghungroo snaps, "You're just an anklet head!"

The girl now mocks, "I shine more than your shell,"
The anklet sparks, encircling feet with spell.
Through midnight mist, the night begins to bend,
A dance forbidden, where honor meets its end.

They tease as wives, the anklet and the bell—
In music's fog, their fates together dwell.

The Drizzle From Your Village

I still recall the rain that kissed your land,
You came, drenched soft, your sari pressed so tight.
Its weave revealed the curves you could not stand,
While thunder danced and veiled the sky with light.

Your village rain insists, it calls my name,
I stepped once in its song, at your request.
With paper boats, I played a fleeting game,
And sailed my thoughts where memories rest.

I'll come again with dreams in golden sails,
Where silence weeps beneath your cloudy eyes.
That rain still speaks in soft and tender tales,
And hides your truth behind the stormy skies.

It mocks me now, returns without your grace—
Your village rain still drips with your lost face.

Sleep has Fled my Village

The sun in your small sky begins to rise,
And lights my fields with warmth it sends afar.
Your moonlight spills across my village skies,
A borrowed glow from where your heavens are.

The nightangle sings within your forest deep,
And mango buds in mine begin to swell.
When night-time folds you softly into sleep,
Dreams bloom in me, of parting I can't tell.

Blind bees from here seek shade in your dark womb,
That darkness feels like home to all my pain.
Your village dusk, so rich with fragrant gloom,
Bathes mine in love like soft, untimely rain.

How shall the spring wind steal your form from me,
When even dust remembers what used to be?

Black Eagle Books

www.blackeaglebooks.org
info@blackeaglebooks.org

Black Eagle Books, an independent publisher, was founded as a nonprofit organization in April, 2019. It is our mission to connect and engage the Indian diaspora and the world at large with the best of works of world literature published on a collaborative platform, with special emphasis on foregrounding Contemporary Classics and New Writing.

www.ingramcontent.com/pod-product-compliance
Lightning Source LLC
Chambersburg PA
CBHW022221090526
44585CB00013BB/942